SU
DIALECT

A Selection of Words and Anecdotes
from Around Sussex

By

Louise Maskill

BRADWELL
BOOKS

Published by Bradwell Books
9 Orgreave Close Sheffield S13 9NP
Email: books@bradwellbooks.co.uk
©Louise Maskill 2012

1st Edition
ISBN: 9781902674339 (Sussex)
Print: Gomer Press, Llandysul, Ceredigion SA44 4JL

Design by: JenksDesign@yahoo.co.uk

ACKNOWLEDGEMENTS

Thanks are due to many people for their generosity and support. Chris Gilbert and Zoe Edwards provided research materials, my partner Tom fed the family so I could read and write, and my children didn't mind too much when I was too busy working to go on the swings.

My father-in-law, born and bred in Bognor Regis, has provided books, encouragement, boundless enthusiasm and has badgered friends and acquaintances on my behalf. My parents and the rest of my family have cheered from a distance, and are looking forward to the Norfolk and Yorkshire editions.

Huge thanks to all of you.

DEDICATION

For Ken, a Sussex man through and through

She reminded herself that Sussex, when all was said and done, was not quite like other counties.

Stella Gibbons, Cold Comfort Farm

INTRODUCTION

Although dialects are still evident in everyday speech from different parts of the country, they are nowhere near as common or as diverse as they used to be. This gradual extinction has been noted and mourned by writers and antiquarians over many years, and huge efforts have been made to capture the colloquial speech of men and women from various parts of the country.

The county of Sussex has been a particular focus for these efforts. Dialect was preserved in some areas well into the twentieth century, helped by the county's relative geographical inaccessibility behind the physical barriers of the Sussex Downs and the ancient forest of the Weald. This book represents a selection of words, phrases and anecdotes gathered from many different sources; one or two are even unique to this collection, contributed by Sussex natives of the author's acquaintance!

The first part of the book is an A to Z of words and phrases arranged with their meanings and a few examples of usage, while the second part contains a collection of anecdotes, stories, rhymes and curiosities, all arranged by theme. Some of the words in the A to Z are now in common use in everyday English, but the aim is to indicate their provenance in the old Sussex dialect. The anecdotes may be long or short, complicated or simple, but all contain genuine examples of Sussex dialect as recorded by historians and collectors over the years. At the very least the stories should raise a smile, but if they also contribute to saving the dialect from total extinction, then so much the better.

A

Abed - in bed
About as common - in reasonable health
Abroad - in all directions, all around
Absit - absent
Ache - to tire of something
Ackle - fit
Adder's spear - a large dragonfly
Adry - thirsty
Afeared - afraid
Aggy - peevish, out of sorts
Agin - close to, up against
All one - all the same
Along of - on account of
Alus - an ale house
Amendment - manure
Ammots or ammuts - ants

You goo down to th' ten-acre field an' spread that amendment abroad, an' peck up them ammut-castes.

Amost - almost
Ampery - weak, unhealthy or rotten
Anywhen or anywhiles - at any time
Appleterre - an orchard
Applety - a loft where apples are stored
Apse - an aspen tree
Arder - an adder
Arney - in a bad temper
Arter - after
Arts and parts - in all directions
Aside - bankrupt

A

Atween or atwixt - between
Ax - ask
Axey or ague - a common and prevalent complaint in many parts of Sussex

Ague, ague, I thee defy,
Three days shiver, three days shake,
Make me well for Jesus' sake!

B

Babbins - wood used for fire-lighting
Bachelor's button - the pink clematis
Backstays, backsters or flappers - wide flat pieces of wood, similar to snow shoes, used by fishermen to cross shingle beaches or soft mud
Backturned - facing away from

'He was backturned when I saw him' - he had his back to me when I saw him.

Backwent - moving away from

'I only saw him backwent' - I only saw him when he was walking away from me.

Bait - afternoon refreshment in the harvest field
Ballies - belly
Balsam - uncomplimentary backchat or remarks
Bannick - a severe beating

B

Bat - a walking stick or other piece of wood
Bat and trap - a team game played on Good Friday
at Burgess Hill and on Brighton Level
Batfowler - one who takes birds at night using a net
on a long pole
Bawl - to read aloud

*Said a mother of her child, kept off school because of illness: 'I
keeps him to his book all the same, and his father likes to hear
him bawl a bit in the evening.'*

Beat the Devil round the gooseberry bush - tell
a long story or rigmarole without much point to it

*An old man in Rye was heard to complain that he didn't think
the new curate was much of a hand in the pulpit, he did beat
the Devil round the gooseberry bush so.*

Beazled - exhausted, worn out, weary
Beever - eleven o'clock luncheon or snack
Beleft - believed
Belikes - very likely
Bellick - to bellow
Bellus - bellows (used in the iron industry or a forge)
**Bendin'- in or Bread-and-cheese-and-beer
Day** - a party held on two of Brighton's fishing
beaches at the start of the mackerel season
Benson's pig - the floor or the ground

*Giving someone 'a close view o' Benson's pig' means to give
them a thrashing.*

B

Bethanks - thank goodness
Bethwine - the wild clematis or traveller's joy (also tom-bacca)
Bettermost - superior or best
Bibber - to shake or rattle, as a window
Bidance - abode, dwelling
Bide - stay, remain
Bilbo - a sheep bow, a Y-shaped wooden frame to hold a sheep's head during shearing
Biscuit - a cake

In Sussex the words biscuit and cake exchange their usual meanings, so that a plum biscuit is a cake made with plums.

Black Ram Night - a celebration of the end of sheep shearing
Blackthorn Winter - a cold spell in early spring when the blackthorn blossom is already out
Bleat - cold
Blobtit or blobtongue - a tell-tale
Blue-bottle - the wild hyacinth
Blunder - the sound of something heavy falling
Bluv - believe
Bob - a beetle
Boco - much, a lot, a large quantity (from the French 'beaucoup')
Bodge - a job carelessly or shoddily done
Bodger - a badger
Borstal or bostal - a steep path, particularly over the Downs
Brake - bracken
Brave, bravely - in good health, prosperous

B

Bread and cheese - hawthorn buds
Bread and cheese friend - a true and trusted friend
Brencheese - bread and cheese
Brish - as quickly as possible
Brown bird - the thrush
Budge - serious or solemn
Bullock - a fat beast of either sex
Bum-freezer - a short coat
Burnish - to grow fat
Buss - a short, heavy, very strong fishing boat characteristic of Hastings

C

Cackleberry - an egg
Cadger - anyone given to begging
Caddling - looking around for odd jobs
Cadey - a hat
Caffincher - the chaffinch
Call over - to abuse or complain about
Callow - smooth or bare
Cant - a strip or division of a field, often used to apportion an expected day's work for a single man at harvest time
Catch hot - to fall ill with a fever
Catch hurt - to have an accident
Caterwise - diagonally
Catterning - the custom of begging for apples and beer on St Catherine's Day
Chance-born or come-by-chance - an illegitimate child
Chank - to chew

C

Charm stuff - medicine for the ague or the axey
Chat - a very small potato
Chavee - a young child
Chee - hen roost
Chipper - lively, cheerful, happy
Chizzly - gritty and harsh on the teeth
Chockly - dry
Chog or shog - the core of an apple
Chop-backs - a derogatory name given to Hastings fishermen by the fishermen of other towns
Chuckle-headed - stupid
Chuff - miserable or surly
Church-cried or church-bawled - having the banns read in church before getting married
Churn owl - the nightjar
Clam - a cold sweat
Clapper - the tongue
Clat - to cut wool and other less savoury matter from a sheep's rear end
Clawneys - family relations or ancestors
Clemmed - hungry or cold
Clemmening - the custom of begging for apples and beer on St Clement's Day, the blacksmith's festival
Clim - to climb, or to hold onto
Clopper or clog boot - a boot with a wooden sole, worn by fishermen
Close - a farmyard
Clung - cold and damp, as in wet washing or cut grass in cold weather
Codger - a miser
Coger or coager - luncheon, usually of bread, cheese and beer

C

Concerned in liquor - drunk
Coolthe - coolness
Crank, cranky - merry, cheerful; also drunk
Crazy - out of order, dilapidated
Create - to make a fuss
Cuckoo gate - a kissing gate
Culver - a pigeon or dove
Cut your stick - be off, be on your way
Curious - unsteady, drunk

D

Dab - a flounder
Dallop - a parcel of tea, packed for smuggling
Dang or dannel - variation of 'Damnation', used as an expletive
Darks - in seafaring or smuggling terms, the nights when there is no moon
Darling or dawlin - the smallest pig in a litter; sometimes also applied to an unhealthy child
Dead alive - dull, heavy or stupid
Deaf adder - a slow worm
Deedy - clever or industrious
Deese or deeze - a place where herrings are dried
Dentical - weak or feeble
Dereaway - thereabouts
Derricking - the technique of hauling goods up cliffs from inaccessible beaches
Devil's children - magpies
Devourous - voracious
Dezzick or duzzick - a day's work
Dinlow - slow-witted
Dish of tongues - a good scolding

D

Dishwasher, dishwipe or dishlick - the pied wagtail
Disremember - to forget
Dobbs or Master Dobbs - a house-fairy who does all sorts of domestic work

'Master Dobbs has been helping you!' - a common expression used when someone has done more work than expected.

Doddle - to tremble or walk unsteadily
Doling - a fishing boat with two masts
Done over - tired out
Dosset or dozzle - a small portion
Down - ill, poorly
Down bed - a bed on the floor
Drackly - directly

When a Sussex man is asked to do something he doesn't want to do, he will answer, 'Drackly.' This means, 'I'll do it when I'm good and ready, and not before.'

Draggle tail - a woman of dubious morals
Druv - driven

A favourite maxim among the stubborn Sussex folk is the assertion that 'I wunt be druv!'

Drythe - a drought or a thirst
Duffer - a peddler
Dumbledore - the bumble bee

Dumbledores are said to have a spear in their tail, but in Sussex a bee is always said to bite, rather than sting.

D

Dunch - deaf, or slow to understand
Dunnamuch - don't know how much
Dunnamy - don't know how many
Dunnick or dunnekin - a privy over an open cesspit
Dursn't - must not, dare not
Dutch cousins - great friends

E

Earsh - a field of stubble
Eddel - rotten
E'enamost - nearly, almost
Effet or affut - a newt
Egger-nogger - sleet (a seafaring term)
Eldern - made of elder wood
Elevener - an early luncheon
Ellar, ellet or eller - the elder tree
Ellum - the elm tree
Ellyinge - solitary, weird or lonely
End on - in a great hurry
Enow or enew - enough
Ernful - sad
Ether - a hedge, or the pliant wood strips wound between stakes to form a hedge

*Fishermen on Hastings beach, c1890
George Woods, East Sussex Library Archive*

F

Faddy - fanciful
Faggot - a good-for-nothing girl
Fail - to fall ill
Fall - autumn
Fambly - family
Fan - to banter or tease
Fanner hawk - a kestrel
Farisees - fairies
Favour - to resemble or look like something
File - a cunning deceitful person
Flap - a large flat mushroom
Fleck - the fur of rabbits or hares
Flew - a kind of fishing net
Flindermouse, flittermouse or fluttermouse - a bat
Flit milk - skimmed milk
Flog - to tire or weary
Flushy - swampy, marshy
Fluttergrub - a man who enjoys working with the earth and getting into a mess
Foredoor - the front door of a house
Fornicate - to dawdle
Foundle - any found thing
Fower - broad pronunciation of 'four'
Frenchy - a foreigner of any country who cannot speak English

When a Swedish vessel was wrecked on the Sussex coast, an old fisherman remarked that the French Frenchys, all in all, were better than the Swedish Frenchys because he could make out what they were driving at. With the others he was all at sea.

F

Fresh - not yet drunk, but rather noisy
Fret - a sea fog
Frit - frightened
Furriner - foreigner; a person from any other county but Sussex (or sometimes even from a neighbouring village)
Fust - first
Futtice - a weasel

G

Gagy - showery
Galleybird or gallowsbird - the woodpecker
Gamel - to romp about
Ganse - hilarity, merriment
Gark - to look at

"We gooes up an' we 'as a gark at 'en."

Gaskin - the wild cherry
Gate - a farmyard
Gay ground - a flower garden
Gazel - a berry, especially a blackcurrant
Geat - a gate
Gentleman - a person who doesn't work for a living; may be applied to women or invalids, and occasionally to animals

"I'm sure I've done all I could for mother; if she isn't a gentleman I'd like to know who is!"

G

Gifts - white specks which appear on the fingernails, supposedly indicating the arrival of a present

A gift on the thumb is sure to come,
A gift on the finger is sure to linger.

Gifty - unwholesome or poisonous
Gigglesome - given to giggling
Gimsy - smartly dressed
Gobbet - a mouthful of something
God Almighty's cow, fly golding or Bishop Barnaby - a ladybird
Gold cup or crowsfoot - the buttercup
Gong farmer - someone who cleans out the privies
Gooden or Goodening - the tradition of going from house to house for gifts on Gooding Day or St Thomas' Day, December 21st
Gooder - an elderly woman doing the rounds of village houses on Gooding Day
Goodman - an old form of address for the master of a house
Goody - the form of address for an elderly widow
Gowk - a cuckoo. May also be applied to a fool
Grabby - grimy, filthy
Grandfather - a daddy-long-legs or cranefly
Greybird - the mistle thrush
Grizzle - fret or complain
Grummut - an awkward boy
Gummut - a lout or stupid fellow
Gurt - great

H

Haboot - a half-boot

Hack - to cough persistently and faintly

Hagridden - to have a nightmare

Hagtracks - circles of coarse green grass, seen in meadows and on the Downs, said to be the tracks of dancing witches or fairies

Haitch - a passing shower

Haitchy - misty, foggy

Hanger - a wood on a hillside

Harbour duck or harbour shark - a Rye term for the harbour man

Harness - temper or mood

Haviler or heaver - a crab

Headache - the corn poppy

Heal - to cover

Hedge-pick or hedge-mike - the dunnock or hedge sparrow

Hedge-pig - the hedgehog

Helve - to gossip

Hem - very, exceedingly; or a term for Hell or damnation

Hern - her own

The possessive pronoun as conjugated in Sussex:
Mine, thine, hisn or hern,
Ourn, yourn, theirn.

Hindsideafore - the wrong way round

Hisn - his own

He as takes what isn't hisn
When he's catched, he'll goo to prison.

H

Hither - the nearer of two things

Hoak - a false excuse or pretence

Hobbledick - a spirit said to live in elder trees, who must be consulted before they are cut down

Hogarves or agarves - may or hawthorn berries (haws)

Hogboat or hoggie - a big fishing boat peculiar to Brighton

Hog-pound - a pig sty

Holy Sunday - Easter Day

Hoveler - a nautical pilot who guides homeward-bound vessels into harbour

Hover - looking cold and shivery; also (of soil) light and friable

Howlers - men and boys who went round orchards wassailing the apple trees

Howsomever - however

Huck - a peapod

Huff - to scold or take to task

Humble cow - a cow without horns

Humbledore or hornicle - a hornet

Hunch - a nudge

Hyme - a wasps' or wild bees' nest

I

Idle - saucy, mischievous or rude

Innards or inwards - the stomach and intestines

Innings - land enclosed from the sea

Itching berries - rosehips

I

Item - a hint or a clue

J

Jack abbler - the crested newt
Jack hearn or erne - heron
Jacket - to flog
Jacob - a magpie
January butter - one of many terms for Sussex mud, renowned for being sticky and heavy, particularly over the Weald
Jawled out - tired, fatigued
Jes - just
Jiggered - surprised
Jipper - gravy
Johnny or Lord John - the ague
Joss up - to mount a horse
Jossing-block - a mounting block
Jostle - to cheat
Journey - a day's work
Jug - a Brighton fisherman
Juggy - a squirrel
Juniper - a flea
Justly - exactly

K

Kellick - an anchor
Kettle broth - bread with salt and pepper in hot water
Keveling - in Brighton, the name given to the skate

K

Kex or kecksies - hogweed, cow parsley and other plants of the same family
Kiddle or kittle - to tickle or tease, or to entice
Kime or kine - a weasel
Kink - to entangle
Kiss me - wild heartsease
Knap, knep or kneb - a small hill
Knucker - a water dragon. One such lived in the knucker hole at Lyminster, near Arundel
Knucker hole - a pond reputed to be bottomless

L

Lag or leg - a long narrow marshy meadow, usually by the side of a stream
Laine - an open tract of arable land
Lamentable - very
Lapsy - slow, lazy or stupid
Last - a quantity of herrings, equal to ten thousand fish
Lavant - an intermittent rushing stream
Lawyer - a long shoot of bramble, thick and vigorous and covered in thorns

'When once a lawyer gets a holt an ye, ye don't easy get shut of 'em.'

Laurence or Old Laurence - a mysterious personage who is supposed to influence people and cause idleness or laziness

'Old Laurence has got a hold o' me.'

L

Lean - unprofitable
Lear - lean, hungry or faint
Learn - to teach
Lent - a loan
Libbet - a short stick thrown to dislodge nuts and so on from trees
Lippy - impertinent
Liver - mood, temper
Liversick - a hangnail on the finger
Loggerhead - a tadpole
Looker - a shepherd or herdsman, employed to look after cattle in the marshes
Long-dog - a greyhound
Lourdy - heavy, sluggish
Loving mud - heavy, sticky mud, characteristic of the Sussex Weald
Lubbock - a big ungainly person
Lurry - to hurry over work and do it in a careless slapdash fashion
Lunnon - London

M

Maid - a term applied to young children of either gender; also the Hastings term for a skate
Magnify - matter, signify
Marbles Day - an old Sussex name for Good Friday, the culmination of the Lent marbles season
Master - the old term applied by a wife to her husband
Maun - must not
Maunder - to mutter or grumble, or wander about in thought

M

Mawk - a girl of dubious morals
Mawkin - a scarecrow
Mayhap - perhaps
Mazed - bewildered, confused
Mermaid's purses - egg cases from the dog fish, washed up on beaches
Middling - a useful word with many meanings, ranging from 'very much' to 'quite well' or 'not at all'. Sometimes used when the speaker may not want to commit himself
Mind - to remember
Mis or Mus - shortened term for Mister
Misheroon - a mushroom
Mistus - the old term for a wife (from 'mistress')
Misword - a cross or angry word
Mockbeggars - a name given to a house which is grand on the outside but dirty and untidy within
Moil - trouble
Moithered - worn out, perplexed
Moggy - a barn owl, or a cat
Monkey's birthday - a day when it rains and the sun shines at the same time
Moonshine - smuggled spirits
Most-in-general - usually
Mousearnickle - a dragonfly
Muddle about - to do a little work
Mudlark - a Rye fisherman
Mullet - a person born and bred in Arundel, so called because of the many mullet fish to be found in the river Arun

N

Nabble - to chatter or gossip
Nary - not any
Naughty man's plaything - the stinging nettle
Near - stingy, mean
Neddie - a warble fly
Nestle - to fidget, or to do a little work in and out of the house
Nettle-spring - nettle rash
News - to tell or disseminate; to news something about
Niff - to quarrel or take offence
Nip - a stingy or mean person
Nipper - a name for the smallest child in a family, or someone who is unusually small for their age
Nohow - unwell, poorly
Notch - a run in cricket

The old countryside custom was to keep tally by cutting notches in a stick.

Nottable - thrifty or industrious
No-ways - in no way
Nubbly - full of small lumps

O

Oakam - nonsense
Obedience - a curtsey or bow
Old father - the person who gives away the bride at her wedding
Old man's beard - wild clematis

O

Oh-be-joyful - whiskey
One - to be good friends

To be at one with someone is to be good friends. To be at two, however, means the pair have quarrelled.

Ore - seaweed washed ashore by the tides
Otherwhere - somewhere else
Otherwhiles - sometimes, occasionally; or otherwise, the rest of the time
Out of kilter - unwell, sickly
Outlandish - foreign, from a different area or town
Over Will's mother's - in the distance, at some unspecified distance away

'It's a bit dark over Will's mother's.'

Owlet - a moth
Owling - smuggling
Ox-steddle - a stall for oxen

P

Packled - speckled
Painful - painstaking
Pandle - a shrimp
Parson rook - the hooded crow
Pathery - silly; applied especially to sheep
Particular - unwell

'He's lookin' very particular; I don't like the look on 'em.'

P

Passel - a flock, or a collection of things
Peaked - fretful or unwell
Peck - a pick axe; also, to use a pick axe
Peert - lively, charming
Peeze - to ooze out or leak
Peg away - to eat or drink voraciously and greedily
Perk up - to toss the head distainfully
Picksome - finicky, dainty
Pilrag - a field that has been ploughed up and then neglected
Pinch Bum Day - 29th May, known in the rest of England as Oak Apple Day or Royal Oak Day
Pithered - gummed up
Pize - expression of surprise or annoyance, often used in questions

'What the pize has that got to do with you?'

Plaguey - troublesome
Planet - a Hastings term for a brief and sudden gale
Platty - uneven, unpredictable; usually said of a crop or harvest
Plaw - a small wood
Plum heavy - a small round cake made of pie crust with raisins or currants inside
Polt - a hard driving blow
Pook or Puck - a fairy name
Poor - thin
Popple - to bubble
Pork bolter - a Worthing fisherman
Pountle - honest and reliable

P

Powd - a boil
Praper - proper, properly
Prensley - presently, soon
Prickleback urchin - a hedgehog
Primed - half drunk, ready to engage in all kinds of mischief
Print moonlight - very clear moonlight, almost as clear as daylight

'Well, he must have been primed to fall into the pond such a night as that was, for t'was print moonlight.'

Pucker - a fuss, in a state of extreme anxiety
Puckstool - a toadstool
Pug - a ferret
Punt - a type of open-decked fishing boat from Hastings
Purty - pretty
Puss net - a tangle of string

Q

Quaint - acquainted, friendly with
Queer - to puzzle over something

'It has queered me for a long time to find out who that man is, and my mistus she's been in quite a quirk over it. He don't seem to be quaint with nobody, and he don't seem to have no business, and for all that he's always to and thro', to and thro', for everlastin'.'

Q

Quick - a useful word with many meanings:
pregnant, alive, to hurry, or (when applied to sands)
insecure and unsafe to walk on
Quiddy? - What do you say?
Quilly - the roughness of the skin produced by cold;
goose flesh
Quilt - to claw and press with the paws, as cats do on
carpets or soft surfaces
Quirk - a fuss, whim or fancy
Quisby - unsettled weather
Quizzing - searching for something

R

Rabbit's meat - wild parsley
Raddles - long supple sticks of green wood
interwoven between upright stakes to make a hedge
Radical - tiresome or disobedient
Rafty - ill-tempered
Ramp - to grow rapidly or luxuriantly
Rathe - early

'I were out rathe in the morning.'

Rattlebone - worn out, falling to pieces
Red herring - a dried herring, as distinct from a
white (fresh) herring
Recollects - memory

'I quite lost my recollects.'

Reek - fog or mist rising from the marshes

R

Reves - rent or tithes

The fishermen at Brighton were liable to pay six mackerel as reves every time they returned from mackerel fishing.

Reynolds or Reynard (often Mus Reynolds or Mus Reynard) - the country name given to a fox

'I thought Mus Reynolds was about last night, the ducks kept all on squacketting so.'

Ride - any bridleway, but generally a green way through woodland
Ringing the bull - a traditional game played in Sussex pubs
Ringle - a small ring, such as that put into the snout of a pig to stop him rooting up the floor of his sty
Ripe - a bank or sea shore
Robbut - rabbit
Rookery - a disturbance or a fuss
Rorty - aggressive, angry
Round frock - a loose tunic or frock of coarse material, generally work by country people over their other clothes. A white round frock is considered to indicate mourning
Rubber - a whetstone
Rubbidge - rubbish
Runaway jack - ground ivy
Rusty - ill-tempered, unruly

S

Sabbed - wet, saturated
Sally - a willow tree
Salts - marshes near the sea, overflowed by the tide
Sare - withered or dry
Sarternoon - this afternoon
Saytered - thoroughly soaked
Scad - the bullace, a wild plum similar to the damson which grows in hedgerows
Scamble - to make a confusion of something
Scar - exposed

'Our house is quite scar to the sea.'

Scoon - to look about
Scorse - to exchange
Scraze - when falling over, to scratch and bruise at the same time

'She was climmin' up after some scads and she fell down and scrazed her knees.'

Scritch owl - a barn owl
Scrouging - pushing
Scutty - a wren (also called a cutty or a kitty)
Sessions - a great deal of fuss
Set - obstinate, self-willed, determined
Shackle - to idle about, to busy oneself doing nothing
Shacky - shabby, ragged
Shatter - a great number or quantity

'There's a tidy shatter o' apples this year.'

S

Shay - a faint ray of light

Sheen - an old steam-driven threshing machine

Sheere-man - a foreigner, from anywhere else apart from Sussex

Sheere-mouse - a field mouse or shrew-mouse. May also be a term of derision for a sheere-man

Sheeres - the Shires; anywhere else in the world apart from Sussex (and, at a push, Kent)

'I don't exactly know the name of the place he's gone to, but I do know 'tis a middling stride into the Sheeres.'

Shell fire - phosphorescent light from rotting matter; also called fairy fire

Shepherd's crown or fairy loaf - a fossilised sea urchin found in chalk

Shim - a glimpse of anything

Shimeroys - gnats or midges

Ship - sheep

Shirty - easily offended

Sussex folk will describe someone who is easily offended as being 'shirty'. A man who has rapidly lost his temper is said to have 'got his shirt out'.

Shog (or chog) - the core of an apple

Shorn bug - a generic term for beetles

In Sussex, if a family is said to eat shorn bugs for dinner, they are in a terrible state of poverty.

S

Short - out of temper, unable to give a civil answer; also, of meat, tender and good to eat

Shruck - shrieked, yelled

Shucky, shuckish - a fisherman's term for unsettled weather

Sidy - surly or moody

Siever - all the fish caught at one tide

Silly Sussex - a scornful name for Sussex folk

Skice - to run quickly and slyly, in order to avoid detection

Skreel - a scream or shriek

Slabby - dirty, wet, slippery, greasy

Slap - in good condition, hale and hearty

Slop - a short full frock of coarse material, worn by men over their other clothes. It reaches the waist, where it is fastened by a band

Smeech or smutch - a dirty black smoke or mist, like the smoke from a snuffed candle

Snag or sneg - the common snail

Snag, snag, put out your horn,
And I will give you a barley corn.

Sniggler - a light frost

Snob - a travelling shoemaker or cobbler

Snottgogs - yew berries

Snuffy - angry

Sodger - soldier; also a red herring

Solly - tottering or unstable

Somewhen - sometimes

Soodling - a slow meandering walk or stroll

S

Sops and ale - a men-only custom from Eastbourne celebrating the arrival of new babies

Spadger - sparrow

Spannelling - making muddy footprints, as does a wet dog

Spartacles - a corruption of spectacles

Spear - the sting of a bee

Sprackish - smart and active

Sprucing - lying, making things up

Spud - a long-handled gardening implement used for weeding, or the hole in a sock where the toe or foot pokes through

Squackett - to quack like a duck

Squimbly - feeling unwell or upset

Squrrl - squirrel

Stabble - to make a floor dirty by walking on it in wet or muddy shoes

Stade - the shore where ships are beached

Stew - a pool in which fish are kept for the table

Stilts - crutches

Foreigners in Sussex may be surprised to hear that an old man or woman is such a complete cripple that they can only walk with stilts.

Stithe - an anvil

Stoache - to trample the ground, like cattle do in wet weather

Stride - a long way, particularly outside Sussex

Strig - the stalk or any flower or plant

Stupe - stupid or dull

Suddent - suddenly

S

Sullage - filth or dirt

Sureleye - a useful word, often added at the end of a sentence for special emphasis

Sushy - dry, in want of water (often applied to gardens or fields)

Sussex pond pudding - a suet pudding with lemon syrup inside

Sussex pudding or hard dick - a mixture of flour and water, boiled until it sets and then eaten cold

Sussex weed - oak trees, grown in profusion in the Weald and used extensively in the shipbuilding industry

Swallocky - the appearance of clouds in hot weather, usually before a thunderstorm

Swelt - hot or faint

Swole - swollen, enlarged

Swymy - dizzy or faint

T

Tachener - a young man employed on a fishing boat

Tag - a sheep in its first year

Tantaddlings - small jam tarts

Taters - potatoes

Teg - a one-year-old lamb

Tell - to count

Telling the bees - a Sussex custom, involving passing on news of births, marriages or deaths to the family's beehives

Tempersome - quick-tempered

Tempest, tempesty - windy and rough weather

T

Tessy - angry
Thick of hearing - slightly deaf
Thisyer - this here
Tight - drunk
Timmersome - timid
Timnails - a vegetable marrow
Tip-tongued - to talk in an affected or posh way
Tissick - a ticklish but persistent cough

Punch cures the gout, the colic and the tissick,
And it is agreed to be the very best of physic.

To rights - perfectly, completely
Tom - any male bird, as in a tom-turkey or a tom-parrot
Tom-bacca - traveller's joy or wild clematis
Tooter - a seaside trader
Tossicated - drunk
Trade - the name given to smuggling
Trapes - to trail or drag along the ground
Tree throwing - felling trees for timber
Tressles - the dung of sheep of rabbits
Trug - a traditional shallow oval basket, originally used as a measure on farms
Truggy - (of weather) bad, dirty
Tubbing - the carriage of contraband goods in a barrel or tub, usually concealed by a top layer of legal goods
Tuck - a pinafore worn by children
Tug - a carriage or cart, usually used for carrying timber
Twet - sweat, perspire

T

Twitten - a narrow path or alley between two walls or hedges
Two - to be at two is to quarrel

U

Unaccountable - a favourite all-purpose word, often used as an adjective by Sussex folk. Often used to mean exceedingly or excessively
Unked - lonely, dreary or dismal, or betokening bad weather
Unlucky - always in mischief
Urchin - a hedgehog
Usage - provisions given to workers over and above their wages
Utchy - cold

V

Valiant - stout, well-built
Varn - bracken
Vent - a place where several roads meet (pronounced 'went')
Vlothered - agitated, flustered
Voller - a fallow field

W

Wapple way or waffle way - a bridle path
Waps - a wasp
Waps-hyme - a wasps' nest
Wapsey - spiteful, waspish
Warp - four herrings, two in each hand, a measure used in the days when fish were counted by hand. Thirty-three warps were reckoned to equal a hundred
Wattle or whattle - a hurdle or fence panel
Weald - the name given to the large woodland area which extends from the Downs
Weeze - to ooze
Went - a crossway, lane or passage
Whiffle - to come in gusts or fits and starts, as in rain
Whist - silent
White herring - a fresh herring, as distinct from a red (dried) herring
Wild - people who live in the Downs always refer to the Weald of Sussex as the Wild, and its inhabitants as the Wild People
Willick - a guillemot; also a wild person, or an Eastbourne fisherman
Willocky - wild with anger
Windshaken - thin, puny, weak
Winterpicks - blackthorn berries
Wrastle - wrestle
Wrockled - wrinkled
Wunt - won't
Wuts - oats

X,Y,Z

Yaffle - the green woodpecker
Yape - to gossip
Yarbs - herbs
Yetner - not nearly

'I be'ant forty year old yetner.'

Zackly - exactly

Fishing boats drawn up on Hastings beach, c1890
George Woods, East Sussex Library Archive

Pronunciation and usage

Like many rural areas, the pronunciation of Sussex dialect words and names was markedly different from their urban or received versions, sometimes resulting in confusion for outsiders. The true Sussex man divides the world into two parts – Sussex (and maybe Kent, at a push), and the rest or the world, which is known as the Sheeres. The term is not restricted geographically – as well as applying to neighbouring counties and other parts of the UK, China and Australia have both been described as in the Sheeres. Foreigners (from anywhere other than Sussex or Kent) are known as Sheere-men, and may not be guaranteed a friendly welcome.

A foreigner (from outside Sussex) once asked a Sussex labourer whereabouts he might find Mr Pocock of Alciston. The local claimed to have no knowledge of such a person: "Never heered an him, and doan know any sich pleace."

The man persisted in his denials until a third party intervened and revealed that the labourer was, in fact, Mr Pocock of Alciston himself. Mr Pocock was unabashed. "Why, you should ha' axed fur Mus Palk of Ahson!" he objected.

The world was indeed a much larger place in years gone by. An old woman of Etchingham was once asked whether she had ever had a sweetheart other than her husband, to whom she had been married for around sixty years.

"I did," she replied.

"And why didn't you marry him?"

"Oh," she said, "he was too outlandish." It turned out he came from the next village, all of two miles away.

Sussex place names ending in 'ly' are often pronounced 'lie', rather than the more usual 'lee'. A pair of old rhyming couplets illustrate this:

Hellingly, Chiddingly and Hoathly,
Three lies, and all of them true.
If in Sussex you be,
Then it's Chiddinglie, not Chiddinglee.

Indeed, the 'eye' pronunciation is also heard in the common use of the word 'sureleye' used in many situations to add particular emphasis to a sentence. This and other pronunciation oddities are described in the following advice to those from foreign parts:

Fetching wood in the snow, near Hastings, c1890
George Woods, East Sussex Library Archive

If true Sussex you would be,
*Say surel**eye**, not surely.*
In names of places stress should dwell
Upon the final syllable.
*Thus, Ardingl**eye** doth well accord*
*With South**wick**, Ber**wick** and Sea**ford**.*

During the nineteenth century there was a fashion for writing poetry in local dialect. Richard Lower, a school master at Chiddingly, wrote a number of dialect poems; this is an extract from *Tom Cladpole's Journey to Lunnon*, published in 1830:

Many long miles I shuffled on,
As fast as I could goo;
At last I gun to feel, ya see,
De haboot ring ma toe.

A liddle aluss stood close by –
Thinks I, I'll go in here
And git, ya see, a coger loike,
Ov good brencheese an' beer.

In Sussex dialect, gender is almost always feminine. There's an old saying: "Everything in Sussex is a *she* except a tom cat, and she's a *he*." However, it can be very difficult to tell a Sussex woman's age or marital status from the term of address applied to her. Single girls were often addressed as 'Mrs', with 'Miss' being reserved for married women as an abbreviation of mistress.

To a husband, his wife is his 'mistus', but at some indeterminate age she becomes 'the old 'ooman', and when she reaches her dotage she may even become 'the old gal'. Elderly or not, it used to be said among old Sussex folk that a rosemary bush in a cottage garden would never flower except where the mistus was the master.

'Middling' is a useful word in Sussex, possessing many different meanings. It may mean 'very much', as in: "He lashed out middling, I can tell ye!" It may mean 'quite well', as in: "She turned out purty middling." It may even mean 'terribly bad', as in: "How was the wedding?" "Middling, thank ye." "What, only middling?" "Yes – you see, the parson he entirely forgot about it, and he'd gone away, so we was forced to wait in church two hours."

'Quick' is another multi-purpose word, with many meanings. It can mean pregnant, or else it may mean alive: "I thought the sheep was dead when I first saw it, but I found it was quick still." It can also mean to hurry: "I'll quick him fast enough if he doesn't quick himself a little more."

When it is applied to the sands of the Sussex beaches, it can also mean unsafe and insecure for walking or riding: "You should not ride on the sands so soon after the tide has turned, for they are sure to be quick and shifting."

Peck is the old Sussex word for a pick axe, but it is also used to refer to the use of such an axe. Such axes were occasionally used as convenient weapons – the following rather confusing witness statement was given in evidence at a trial for manslaughter, where one man had apparently killed another with his pickaxe.

"You see, he pecked he with a peck, and he pecked he with a peck, and if he'd pecked he with his peck as hard as he pecked he with his peck, he would have killed he, and not he he."

Apple pressing near Hastings, c1890
George Woods, East Sussex Library Archive

Traditions and Customs

Foreigners (folk from neighbouring counties) would often refer to Sussex people in scornful terms, calling them "silly Sussex" and laughing up their sleeves at their odd customs. However, among themselves Sussex folk are proud of their intelligence and resourcefulness. Indeed, the term is thought to derive from 'saelig', an Anglo-Saxon word meaning holy, blessed or good. Saelig Sussex therefore means "The Holy Land of the

Market gardeners taking a break, Worthing, c1900
West Sussex County Library Service

South Saxons," so called because of the county's many churches and good people.

Silly or not, Sussex folk are well known for being stubborn. It is said that Sussex itself is pig-shaped, with the snout at Rye in the east, the legs at Beachy Head and Selsey Bill and the rear at Uppark in the west, and Sussex folk match their county in terms of their pig-headedness. It is well known that a Sussex man "wunt be druv"; indeed, W Victor Cook celebrated this maxim in his 1914 poem:

Some folks as come to Sussex,
They reckons as they know
A durn sight better what to do
Than simple folks, like me and you
Could possibly suppose.
But them as comes to Sussex,

They mustn't push and shove,
For Sussex will be Sussex,
And Sussex won't be druv!

The 29th May, which used to be known throughout England as Oak Apple Day (or Royal Oak Day), commemorating the date of Charles II's triumphant return to London and the restoration of the English Monarchy in 1660.

In Sussex, however, it was known rather more irreverently as Pinch Bum Day, in memory of Colonel William Carless who hid with King Charles in the Royal Oak at Boscobel in Shropshire, and had to keep pinching His Royal Highness on his noble posterior to keep him awake and stop him falling out of the tree. Sussex folk would also chastise those who did not 'sport their oak' (wear a sprig of oak or an oak apple) by slashing the backs of their legs with stinging nettles.

The Sussex countryman's traditional attire was the old round frock or smock, which was a cause of some pride. Many were reluctant to give it up in the changing times, even under some pressure from family and friends.

William Shier, an old man from Harting near Petersfield, was very attached to his old-fashioned garb, but his daughter worked in the town and was ashamed of his country clothing. One Sunday she hid his smock. When he failed to find it in its usual place he despaired, but luckily his daughter was on hand and presented him with a fine new coat, which he put on with a great deal of reluctance and after a lot of persuasion. The family were finally able to set off for church in the village.

A shepherd in a traditional frock, c1912
West Sussex County Library Service

However, he was not happy, and later reported: "I were so ashamed of 'un, when we cum to Harting, I took un off and walked in my shirtsleeves pertendin' I were too 'ot."

Bees are the focus of much Sussex folklore. 'Telling the bees' is an old custom which involves informing the family's bees of any births, marriages or deaths. A member of the family must approach the hives and knock three times with the back door key, chanting "The master is dead", or "The mistress has a baby son", or whatever is appropriate. In some areas the custom is to tie a black crêpe bow on each hive in the case of a death in the family. If these courtesies are not followed, the tradition goes, the bees will fly off or die.

An old man of Crowlink, near East Dean, was asked if he had heard of the custom.

"Well, I 'adent afore my old dad died. He kept bees. And I was a-going down the village street when a man said,

"Have you told his bees?" No, I says, I ain't. I've got enough to do without a-telling of his bees. The man replied, "If you had a told them I would have bought 'em, but they won't be no good now." And they weren't – they all died."

Gooding or Goodening was a Sussex tradition whereby the elderly women of a parish would travel from house to house on St Thomas' Day, December 21st, asking for gifts or 'goods' to help them through the festive season to come. Everyone would give according to their trade or their means – the miller would give a little bit of flour, the butcher a scrap of beef and so on, while from those not in trade a donation of money was expected. Widows would get a double ration.

When the Gooders had done the rounds of the local houses they would move to the church, where legacies or collections were doled out. In some places the women had to bring a small offering in exchange for their goods – an evergreen twig or a small branch from a tree.

When Dr JC Sanger, of Seaford in Sussex, was serving as Government Surgeon at the Cape of Good Hope in the mid nineteenth century, he was called to the house of an English settler. He arrived at teatime, and was asked to join the family at their meal. Sitting down at the table he said, "You come from Sussex."

"Yes," said his hosts, "from Herstmonceux, but how did you know that?"

"Because you have got plum-heavies for tea," said the doctor, "which I never saw but when I have been visiting in Sussex."

The village of Ditchling, just north of Brighton, is famous for its witch, who features in various stories. She apparently lived in a cottage called Jack O'Spades on Ditchling Common, and in one story she is credited with the ability to change into a hare. One night she did this, but she was attacked by a gang of man with dogs and bitten on the leg before she managed to escape by jumping through the window of her cottage. The next morning she was seen nursing her leg, or (in another version of the tale) going to one of the village grandmothers to have it bandaged.

Another tale relates how the witch had the power to hold up work on the local farms by stopping carts as they passed her cottage. No matter how hard the horses pulled, the cart wouldn't move until the witch let it go. However, one day she was foiled by a local carter who 'knew':

"The men 'ud beat the hosses an' they'd pull an' they'd tug, but the waggon wouldn't move, an' the ol' witch 'ud come out a-laughin' an' a-jeerin' at 'em, an' they couldn't get on till she let 'em.

"But there wor a carter wot knew, an' he guessed he'd be even wid the ol' witch, so he druv he's waggon before her door, an' then it stopped, an' the horses they tugged, an' they pulled, an' they couldn't move it nohow, an' he heard this ol' witch a-laughin' in the cottage.

"Then this carter what knew, he took out a large knife an' he cuts notches on the spokes, an' there wor a screechin' an' a hollerin' inside, an' out come the ol' witch a-yellin' an' sloppin' blood, an' for every notch on the spokes there wor a cut on her fingers."

Charcoal burners near Hastings, c1890
George Woods, East Sussex Library Archive

This put a stop to the witch's mischief, but just how the carter 'knew' is a mystery which has never been solved.

The knucker that lived in knucker hole, in the water meadows at Lyminster near Arundel, was causing terrible trouble feeding on cattle, horses and the occasional person when he could get them. The Mayor of Arundel offered a reward for anyone who would despatch the beast, and Jim Puttock, a local man from Wick, took up the challenge.

He prepared and cooked a huge Sussex suet pudding, hauling it to the knucker hole on a cart (or tug) pulled by a team of horses. The local people stood and watched from a safe distance as brave Jim approached the knucker lounging in his pool. A local hedger takes up the tale:

And ole Knucker sees thisyer tug a-coming, and he sings out, affable-like, "How do, Man."

"How do, Dragon?" says Jim.

"What you got there?" says Dragon, sniffing.

"Pudden," says Jim.

"Pudden?" says Knucker. "What be that?"

"Just you try," says Jim.

And he didn't want no more telling – pudden, horses, tug, they was gone in a blink. Jimmy ud agone, too, only he hung on to one o' they trees what blew down last year.

But the knucker's eyes were bigger than his stomach, and before long he was roaring and bellowing in agony. After calmly eating his own dinner Jim returned to see what the matter was. The old hedger again:

When he sees en coming, ole Knucker roars out, "Don't you dare bring me no more o' that 'ere pudden, young marn!"

"Why?" says Jim. "What's matter?"

"Colly wobbles!" says Dragon. "Do set so heavy on me I can't stand un, nohows in de wurreld!"

"Shudn't bolt it so," says Jim, "but never mind, I got a pill here, soon cure that."

"Where?" says Knucker.

"Here," says Jim. And he ups with an axe he'd held behind his back and cuts off his head.

The water of the Lyminster knucker hole is still reputed to have magical properties; within living memory a man used to come to the pool and fill little bottles with water, which he then sold as a cure for all ills.

The Village Pub

*Locals outside the Jolly Fisherman pub at Sidlesham,
near Chichester, c1905*
West Sussex County Library Service

A Sussex man is never drunk. He might be a little fresh (translation: not drunk, but rather noisy) or he might have had a little beer (far too much beer). He might have half a pint otherwhile (meaning he's a habitual drunkard). He might be none the better for what he took (which is to say he's much the worse for it), or he might be no-ways tossicated (completely plastered). However much he's had, though, he will declare that he hasn't had more than a pint, and all his friends will agree with him. He might be

51

primed, curious, tight, cranky or concerned in liquor, but drunk? Never!

From Ash Wednesday until Good Friday, men all across Sussex would cast aside all their other pub games and bring out their prize marbles, competing in teams across the county until Good Friday (or Marbles Day) when the local finals would be played, often in the porch of the church (or the churchyard if the weather was fine). The games finished on the dot of twelve noon, when the mid-day service would commence in the church; if any games continued after that time, it was quite legitimate for opposing players to jump on the marbles with cries of "Goblins!", "Scrabbles!" or "Smugs!", claiming them as their own.

The game of Fat was played every Sunday morning in the Trevor Arms in Glynde, near Lewes. It never caught on anywhere else; the following description of the rules, provided by an elderly player of the game, may give a clue as to why.

"Fat? Well, it's nines and fives. You've got the ten wallah and the eighteen wallah, which is the five and the nine of the suit you've made trumps. If you made clubs trumps, the five of clubs was ten and the nine of clubs was eighteen. That's how you peg it, on the peg board you see. And you peg eighty-eight. After you've finished your hand you count up. Ten is ten and you make eighty-eight of it all the time, see. It's an interesting game. I used to like a game of Fat. Nobody can play it now."

Loading the hay at Amberley, near Worthing, c1890
West Sussex County Library Service

Len Page, one of the last true Sussex thresher-men, remembered his old mother fondly. After a fair quantity of good brown ale with friends in a village inn he waxed lyrical about her, but he remembered deceiving her too – an act which he regretted.

"She were a good ol' mother to me," he said, "but I deceived 'er, y'know. Yaas, I alwis kep' one secret from 'er right up to the day she died. She 'ad a favourite canary what went and died – well, 'e didn't die in a manner of speaking 'cos I killed 'im. I was only a nipper at the time and we 'ad bin readin' at school about laburnum seeds bein' pisenous, and kid-like, y'know, I thought I'd like to try it out. So I saved some well-harvested seed off a bush in the garden, chopped it up and wopped it in with the ol' canary's feed. Next mornin', my bwoy, he was layin' on the floor of the cage wid 'is toes turned up. That was pisen all right – 'e was dead as mutton. Gaugh, the ol' lady wasn't 'arf upset. 'Twere a shame really, but I didn't think it would work out just like that. She never did find out 'ow it 'appened."

Later in the same afternoon, after a few more pints of mild and stricken with remorse about the murdered canary, Len set off to find his mother's grave accompanied by his friends Bob and 'Arry. Arriving at the churchyard in the fading light of early evening, the three men set about locating the grave in the overgrown churchyard.

"'Twas around this side somewhere," Len offered. "It 'ad a dove carved on the 'eadstone for Peace, I think."

After a bit more searching Len found the place. "'Ere 'tis! 'Ere 'tis!" he called, and the three men stood with caps in hands looking at the faint weather-worn inscription in the stone: 'Martha Page. Departed this life April 20th, 1919.'

"There y'are, look'ee," murmured Len. "There's th' ol' dove with an olive branch in 'is beak."

'Arry stirred and bent forward to look more closely. "Are you sure, Leonard," he said, "it 'en't a canary wid a sprig o' laburnum?"

Children and Families

Skipping rhymes are as old as the hills and each area of the country has its own versions, sometimes harking back to ancient traditions, perhaps even to pagan rites and celebrations. Community skipping used to take place on Good Friday in many Sussex towns and village, persisting in Brighton up to the outbreak of World War II. One of the most common Sussex rhymes was:

Jam, jam, strawberry jam,
Tell me the name of my young man.
A, B, C, D, …

As the alphabet starts the pace of the rope is picked up, and the letter when the skipping breaks down is the first letter of the name of the young man who will become that particular girl's sweetheart.

Children had their own counting rhymes, often sung in the school-yard over skipping ropes. One such was collected in Sussex in the 1930s:

Ena, deenah, dinah, doe,
Catterah, wheelah, whiler, whoa,
Coram, doram, pullem, flea.

A young Sussex boy was enrolled at the local evening school, but usually failed to attend. When questioned, he gave the reason that he was afraid the farisees would interrupt him on his way home. His mother backed him up, saying that he was "that timmersome that he couldn't abear to go out after dark."

Small boys in Sussex had a strict code of conduct when it came to birds, particularly which ones were fair game and

The High Street in Steyning, near Worthing, c1880
West Sussex County Library Service

which were entitled to protection from harm:

Robins and wrens
Are God Almighty's friends;
Martins and swallers
Are God Almighty's scholars.

Children who lived on farms or in rural communities were usually involved in all aspects of the agricultural year. Boys too little to work elsewhere were often employed on farms as birdscarers, protecting the crops from marauding flocks. It was solitary work; perhaps this rhyme was made up by a lad whiling away the hours in a lonely field:

Shoo all away, shoo all away,
And don't come back no more today.
For if you do, I'll up with me clappers,
And knock you backards.

Children sitting on a gate at Durrington in Worthing, c1914
West Sussex County Library Service

However, anyone who has ever employed small boys to perform some duty will recognise the truth in this old Sussex saying:

One boy is a boy. Two boys is half a boy. Three boys is no boy at all.

When the peas from the harvest had been shelled, children played a game with the empty pea-pods or hucks:

Pea-pod hucks, twenty for a pin.
If you don't like 'em, I'll take 'em back agin.

A pedlar boy used to travel about the Sussex country selling cheap brooches and ornaments. One day he turned up with half a dozen onions in his basket along with the jewellery. When asked whether he had started selling vegetables along with his usual wares, he replied, "No, but I scorsed away a pair of diamond earrings for these few onions with a lady down at the cottage yonder."

Farming and the Land

A muddy Sussex road near Hastings, c1890
George Woods, East Sussex Library Archive

Sussex mud is legendary. It is well known to be an especially viscous and sticky sort of mud, particularly across the Weald, and is generally considered to be far superior to anything that other counties can produce.

There are many Sussex stories involving mud. Legend has it that the women and beasts of Sussex have particularly long legs, developed because of the effort of striding through the glutinous stuff: "Why is it that the oxen, the swine, the women and all other animals, are so long-legged in Sussex? May it be from the difficulty of pulling the feet out of so much mud by the strength of the ankle that the muscles get stretched, as it were, and the bones lengthened?"

One of the best known tales, often repeated and connected with various parts of the county, concerns a man who was walking along a muddy lane and came across a hat lying on the ground. He stooped to lift it up, and was surprised to find a head beneath it. Being a polite sort of fellow he enquired after the health of the head's owner, commenting that he must be finding his present situation a little uncomfortable.

"Nay," came the reply, "not nearly so uncomfortable as the man whose shoulders I'm standing on, nor yet the horse that he is riding."

Sussex folk have a wide and descriptive vocabulary for classifying the mud of their county. Mud may be clodgy (muddy and wet), gawm (sticky and foul-smelling) or slabby (sticky, slippery and greasy). Gubber is a particularly unpleasant type of black mud made of rotting organic matter, while sleech is river sediment sometimes used as manure. Slob is thick mud, but slab is the thickest sort; in contrast, slurry is diluted mud, saturated with water. An ike is a mess or area of mud, while a slough is a muddy hole and a swank is a bog.

Sheep are an integral part of the upland rural scene; generations of shepherd have trodden the grass of the

Downs to tend their flocks. Some West Sussex shepherds counted their sheep in pairs as they ran them into the fold, rather than singly as in other regions. As the pairs of sheep ran past the shepherd would count them in as follows:

One-erum, two-erum, cock-erum, shu-erum, sith-erum,
Sath-erum, wineberry, wagtail, tarrydiddle, den

Since they were counted in pairs, arriving at den meant the shepherd had counted twenty sheep. A notch would be made on the shepherd's tally stick, and the counting would begin again.

Other areas of the county had their own counting rhymes – this one goes up to twenty, with a clear reminder to tally (or cut a notch on the stick) when twenty is reached:

Wintherum, wontherum, twintherum, twontherum, wagtail,
Whitebelly, coram, dar, diddle, den,
Etherum, atherum, shootherum, cootherum, windbar,
Bobtail, inadik, dyadic, bumpit, ecack-tally.

Sussex shepherds were highly particular about female visitors to their lambing folds. One said, "Boss's wife be too fond o' poken' 'bout here. If I got a ewe as wants a doctor, I fastens t'wattle tight. I wunt have women lookin' on while I be doctor, fur 't'int decent!"

Old Dick was a well-known local character around Horsham, a simpleton whose eccentric and amusing escapades and sayings were passed around with a great deal of glee. Once a farmer paid Dick to work on his farm for a few days, helping with the sheep. After a while the farmer came to check on what Dick was up to.

A shepherd with his dog and flock on the South Downs above Steyning, near Worthing, c1910
West Sussex County Library Service

"Have you counted those sheep yet, Dick?" he asked.

"Yep," came the reply, "I counted 'em all but one, but 'ee run about so much, I couldn't count of 'ee."

One evening Bob and Len, two old Sussex countrymen, sat comfortably drinking tea on the steps of Len's caravan, watching as rooks flew back to roost in the tree in Stanmer Park, between Falmer and Coldean. Len watched the birds with a thoughtful air.

"Look at they ol' rooks," he said. "They've bin up on Mus Huxham's top piece since 'ar-parst-seven s'mornin. He drilled it with winter wuts las' wik an' they an' arf give it socks. They're up there every day reg'lar as clockwork. Wal – you work it out for y'self. Look at 'em, there mus' be five or six 'undred birds up there and if they work back three

Two farm labourers takin' a bit o' coger,
near Hastings, c1890
George Woods, East Sussex Library Archive

or four ounces o' grain each that's the best part of a
'undred weight o' seed corn goin' 'ome to Stanmer Park
every night. Makes y'think, dunnit?"

Later on, after a good few pints of brown ale at the inn,
Len's stories were starting to get a little more fruity. "Did
I ever tell y' about the time I wuz going' t'work and took
a short cut 'cos I wuz late? I wuz gettin' over an ol' stile at
the end o' Church Lane an' just as I got astride av it the
bleddy board broke. Down I went like a ton o' taters right
on top the centre post. Gaugh! That caught me right
where the monkey keeps 'is nuts, and the wax flew out my
ear-'oles, bwoy, like pellets out av a tater-gun."

One September morning somewhere around 1911, a
shepherd near Falmer noticed that one of his tegs was

missing from the flock. The matter was reported to the police since a sheep had also gone missing the previous year and sheep stealers were suspected, and the local constable and the farmer followed boot- and hoof-prints across laines and down tracks to a heavily overgrown area of gorse. After quizzing about fruitlessly they gave up the search and returned home, despatching a local boy to make a more thorough search of the area while they themselves made a tour of the local butchers' shops to see if any mutton had been offered to them. The boy, Jim Copper, takes up the tale.

"So I went home and put on some old clothes, for I know what bush-whacking is. All dressed up and somewhere to go, I cut off a crust of brencheese and not quite knowing what I should come up against I thought I would take my heavy weeding spud with me. Then all away out I goes for High Barn.

"Well now, let's find this mutton. I thought my best way would be to take it in cants of about ten to twelve feet wide, giving me five or six feet either side which would be quite as far as I should be able to see. So in I goes, and as I went along I put my cap, handkerchief and a bit of paper on the highest bush to give me a guide back.

"I struggled on for'ard and back a few times, shifting my guide marks each time, and I had done about five wents when I came across a rather big rabbit hole or it might have been a fox earth. I peeked in and saw a small piece of wool, and with my spud I raked out quite a lot of wool and some small bones, the skin and offal of the sheep we had lost previous.

"Finding it raised my hopes considerably, and away I goes again for'ard and back again until I had struggled through the whole patch but found nothing more to my advantage. I was making my way to Iford side when I noticed a few threads of wool clinging to a high branch of brush, not feeling very keen I just went in to have a look and when I got to it I saw a little bit more further on, so I struggled on and kicked against something bulky. Clearing away the brambles with my spud, there sure enough was what I was looking for, the dead sheep – or what was left of it. How I missed it in my to and fro bouts I can't understand.

"I left it just as I had found it and came out on the turf wondering what was best to do. I decided to hang on till someone came along. I had not long to wait, for on looking up I saw PC Wills and an Inspector of the Brighton Police. The Inspector said to me in a very gruff voice, 'Well sonny, have you found the sheep? You look more like a sheep stealer yourself than anything else.'

"I didn't appreciate the greeting, so I said, 'Yes I have. That's what I was sent here for. I have found two. The one we lost twelve months ago and the one that was stolen last night – or what's left of it. And if you can find the missing parts you'll have the sheep stealer.'

"PC Will said, 'You ain't sprucing, are you, Jim?'

"'No,' I said, 'if you come with me I will take you to it.'

"So we went round and when we got there I went barging in an told them to follow. As we were ploughing through I heard the Inspector say, 'This is tough travelling, Wills.'

"I looked round and said, 'Yes, I reckon you would look

like a couple of sheep stealers if you had two hours of it like I have.'

"No comment."

The sheep stealers were never caught – the chief suspect, one Irish Mike, got wind of the police investigation in the local pub and prudently disappeared off to Brighton. Jim was phlegmatic, however:

"If we should have caught the culprits red-handed, the penalty for sheep-stealing in the old days was hanging by the neck. But we tripped up and lost the lot. But still, there it is, it's just one of those things that do happen. And I didn't get the £10 reward."

Foxes were (and still are) a real and present danger to smallholders in rural Sussex. As in many other areas, country folk had their own names for them. When a traveller in Sussex was told that "Mus Reynolds" had paid a visit to a farm the previous evening, he assumed that this individual must be a family friend and expressed a hope that he had been favourably received. "He helped hisself," came the miserable reply, followed by an explanation that Reynolds was the old name for a fox, and this particular Mus Reynolds had made free with the farmer's poultry.

The following tale was told by a Sussex labourer, recounting one of many tales about the small folk or 'farisees' that lived in and around Sussex.

"I've heard my father say that when he lived over the hill, there was a carter that worked on the farm along with him, and no one couldn't think how t'was that this here man's horses looked so much better than what anyone else's did.

Bringing home the hay, near Hastings, c1890
George Woods, East Sussex Library Archive

I've heard my father say that they was that fat they couldn't scarcely get about, and this here carter he was just as much puzzled as what the rest was.

"So cardinley he laid himself up in the stable one night to see if he could find the meaning an't. And he hadn't been there very long, before these here liddle farisees they crep in at the sink hole; in they crep, one after another; liddle tiny bits of chaps they was, and each an 'em had a liddle sack of corn on his back, as much as ever he could carry.

"Well, in they crep, on they gets, up they clims, and there they was, just as busy feeding these here horses, and prensley one says to t'other, he says, "Puck," says he, "I twets, do you twet?" And thereupon, this here carter he jumps up and says, "Dannel ye," he says, "I'll make ye twet afore I've done wud ye!" But afore he could get anigh 'em they was all gone, every one an 'em.

"And I've heard my father say that from that day forard this here carter's horses fell away, till they got that thin and poor that he couldn't bear to be seen along wid 'em, so he took and went away, for he couldn't abear to see hisself no longer, and nobody ain't seen him since."

Another farming tale illustrates the inventive and creative lengths that some Sussex farmers would go to if the welfare of a favourite animal was in jeopardy. This story was overheard on a bus journey by Bob Copper, the prolific collector of songs and stories from all parts of Sussex.

"Years gone by there was a farmer 'ere 'ad a favourite milking keow. A Jersey I think 'twas, name of Daisy, and 'e used to graze it in that 'ere medder. Wal, bye 'n' bye there came the day one summer when the ol' keow wen an' planted 'er 'oof plumb clean in the middle of a 'ornet's nesty. Wal, they ol' 'ornets didn't think a lot to that and they set about the ol' gal good an' proper. They stung 'er all round one of 'er ear-'oles an' the side of 'er 'ead blew up like a thanksgiving pumpkin at 'arvest time. She were took middlin' sick, look. 'Er milk dried up, she went awf 'er feed an' she couldn't see out of 'er eyeballs 'er 'ead were so swole.

"O' course, you 'ad a job to git 'old of a vet that time o' day, so the ol' farmer wopped a bleddy great linseed poultice on the side of 'er 'ead an' lashed it on with strips o' sackin' and binder twine. Then 'e let 'er bide quiet fer a day or two an' after a while she began to git a li'l better. But when 'e went an' took the poultice awf, 'er ear came away along with it leaving 'er ear-'ole open to the weather.

"That were a 'orrible mess at fust, but after a wik or two when the 'air 'ad began to grow over the scar she didn't look too bad. Just a li'l lop-sided, you might say. But the main trouble was that the rain used to trickle down inside 'er 'ead and cause all manner o' trouble.

"Wal, the ol' farmer 'e didn't know what to do fer the best. It simmed a pity to 'ave to put 'er down just 'acause she'd only got one ear, for she was otherwhiles in good 'eart. So 'e went down to ol' Charlie 'Obbs the saddler and 'arness-maker and, "Charlie," 'e sez, "I wants you to make me a leather ear for my ol' Daisy."

"Charlie turns round an' 'e sez, "What, fer yer ol' woman?"

"The ol' farmer turns round an' 'e sez, "No, fer my ol' milkin' keow o' course," 'e sez.

"Charlie turns round an' sez, "What sort o' thing 'ave ye got in mind then?"

""Wal, look'ee, I've drawed it all out on this 'ere bit o' paper. All you warnt is a piece o' soft leather about like the tongue out o' yer boot only a li'l bit bigger somewhat, and some leather lacing to tie 'er on with an' make fast. I be sure you kin do it."

"An' that is just what ol' Charlie 'Obbs done. That ol' keow wore that leather ear for several years right up to the time when she keeled over. An' that medder's bin called 'Obbs's Ear ever since."

A rural scene in the Hastings area, c1890
George Woods, East Sussex Library Archive

A final farming tale was recounted by an old man who recalled his dealings with a "rorty gander" and a peculiarly effective method for dealing with the creature.

"I wuz later for work one mornin' when I wuz carter-boy, an' th' ol' carter give me a roustin' an' asked me where I'd bin.

""Wal," I said, "I couldn't come thro' th' farm-yard, that ol' gander there chased me out on it an' I 'ad t' goo roun'. That took me another ten minutes even tho' I did run all th' way. An' I didn' even stop to pant!"

""You be'ant afear'd of a gander, be y' boy?" 'e 'ollered.

""Yes I be," I said. "'E come at me with 'is wings outstretched, 'is beak a'gapin' an' 'issin' like a snake. Anyway 'e be bigger 'an I be."

""You meet me by de farm gairt t'morrer mornin' at quarter t' six," 'e said. "I'll show you 'ow t' deal wid dat customer."

"So next mornin' I does as 'e said, an' in thro' the gate we gooes t'gether. Sure 'nough th' ol' gander comes acrawss at us – 'alf runnin' an' 'alf flyin' 'e wuz – wings out an' mouth open. I gits roun' behin' th' ol' carter out th' way a bit smartish.

"Wal, th' ol' carter 'e wuz an ol' bacca chower – y' never see 'im without 'is chow an' 'e could squirt 'is bacca-juice seven or eight foot an' 'it a 'orse-fly on a cow-turd, 'e could. Wal, as I say, when that ol' gander come up all gapin' th' ol' carter took 'is quid out of 'is gob – 'twas bigger 'an a pigeon's egg – an' 'e popped it right down that ol' gander's throat. Then 'e grabbed 'is beak close an' 'eld on with both 'ands.

"That ol' gander flapped roun' an' roun' like a jack-her'n in a fish-pond. But th' ol' carter 'eld onto 'im an' 'e 'ad no option only swaller it. You could watch it goin' down inside 'is neck like a 'tater inside a worsted stockin'.

"When th' ol' carter eventually let goo 'e went away charkin' an' coughin' with 'is wings trailin' along on th' groun'.

""Dat's de way t' treat a rorty gander," 'e said. "You wunt 'ave no more trouble wid 'e.""

In the 1930s, two spinster ladies moved into a house in a Sussex village. The house and garden had stood empty and neglected for four years, but the locals were very much aghast at their 'furriner' ways, especially their gardening practices. They asked a village labourer to work for them and help them clear the garden. He was not keen.

"Wanted me to pull out all the rubbidge," he grumbled. "I always digs 'em in, I told 'em. That's how we do's it in West Sussex. It's as good as amendment for the ground.

"But no, they would have it all out an' lay the kecksies an' lily on one side an' bury all the other rubbidge along o' some stuff as they bought at the chymist's. I told 'em they'd better dig it theirsens, an' off I went."

Likewise, when they planted their potatoes at the bottom of a trench in the ground, their neighbours were amazed and confused. One old man offered them "a lent o' my debber" to help them make individual holes, but they refused in their tip-tongued way and went on planting in their trench.

However, they seemed to get results; in a year when fruit crops were scarce, a village woman noted: "Them furriners have got a nice shatter of apples on their trees. But they're unaccountable deedy. Apples is very platty this year."

Later in the year, the same village labourer who had refused to clear the rubbidge from the garden was asked how his potatoes were doing.

"Blighted like everyone else's", he replied shortly. "'Ceptin' them deedy furriners. Their taters looks fine. I s'pose they're not so sushy down there as we are – terrible sushy, our gardens are. But they've got a nice shatter o' apples an' pears, an' their taters looks unaccountable fine. Luck, I s'pose, for it's not the way they planted 'em!"

Fishing, Smuggling and the Sea

Sussex has a rich maritime heritage. From Bosham and the Witterings in the west to Camber in the east, the coast and the sea have provided a living for generations of families, who have fished and worked the shores as well as engaging in other more nefarious practices involving dark nights and barrels of contraband goods.

A fisherman in traditional clothing on Hastings beach, c1890
George Woods, East Sussex Library Archive

Bendin-in, or Bread-and-cheese-and-beer day, was the name given to a party thrown by the masters of the Brighton fishing fleet for their men to mark the start of the mackerel season. The meal of bread, cheese and beer was served to the fishermen, their

72

wives and families, and then the folded fishing nets were blessed by the parish priest. A special benediction was also used on the first casting of the nets from the vessels, as the barrel-floats bobbed ready to be hauled back in with the catch:

Watch, barrel! Watch!
Mackerel for to catch.
White may they be like a blossom on a tree.
God sends thousands, one, two, three.
Some by their heads, some by their tails,
God sends thousands and never fails.
There they goes then: God Almighty
Send us a blessing it is to be hoped.

Bognor seafront from the pier, 1890
West Sussex County Library Service

Times were when everyone in Sussex who lived within reach of the coast was in some way connected with smuggling – or 'the Trade', as it was known. These activities were never regarded as dishonest, being

Fishermen and their families on Hastings beach, c18 George Woods, East Sussex Library Archive

instead viewed as work carried out in answer to the introduction of unpopular taxes which were seen as an infringement of liberty. Labourers were always ready to help whenever the darks fell, farmers allowed their horses to be borrowed for the night, and vicars made no mention of mysterious barrels which took up temporary residence in church vaults. Even the Excise men sometimes collaborated for a price, but when disagreements arose and men came to blows the doctor tended to wounds for nothing, and never enquired about the provenance of the dallops of tea or kegs of brandy which appeared on his doorstep at daybreak. Rudyard Kipling, who lived in the heart of smuggling country, knew very well that the policy was to "watch the wall, my darling, while the gentlemen go by."

Some villages were particularly well known for their collaboration with the smugglers. In Yapton villagers would leave their doors open so that smugglers could make a fast getaway if the Excise men were on their tail. This is still remembered today when careless folk may well be berated for leaving doors standing open with the cry: "Close that door! Do you come from Yapton?"

Churches and Religion

Parsons and clerks were often complicit in smuggling escapades, but sometimes they were not included in the nefarious dealing and then great pains had to be taken to keep them in ignorance of the shady activities going on under their noses. At one time Hove and Preston, two parishes near Brighton, were served by a single clergyman who preached at each place on alternate Sundays. One Sunday he arrived at Hove to find that no preparations had been made for the service.

He sought out the parish clerk and enquired as to the reason, but was politely informed, "This is Preston Sunday, sir."

"No, you are wrong. I preached there last Sunday."

The clerk was insistent, but the vicar remained firm. After an increasingly indignant exchange, with neither side backing down, the clerk eventually became exasperated.

"Look," he said, "you can't preach here today. The church is full o'tubs, and the pulpit is full o'tea!"

Parsons and clerks worked closely together in aid of the spiritual wellbeing of their parishioners, but they did not always chime perfectly together. Clerks were often relatively uneducated men from the local area, but part of their responsibility was to make announcements in church.

In performing this duty they often tried to adopt a serious and self-important air, occasionally with unfortunate results. One rainy Sunday a Downland clergyman suffered an accident on the way to church, falling from his horse and saturating himself so thoroughly that he needed to return home. His clerk was left to announce that because of a slight accident the parson would be unable to preach.

Accordingly, after prayers had been concluded the clerk arose with an air of great gravity, and announced, "Ye be to goo now. Passon ain't a-gooin' ter praich to-dey acause he's wet 'isself."

A Sussex country vicar was remonstrating with one of his parishioners for abusing the parish clerk beyond reasonable bounds. The parishioner gave the following answer: "You be quite right, sir, you be quite right. I'd no ought to have said what I did, but I don't mind telling you to your head what I've said a-many times behind your back – we've got an good shepherd, I says, an axcellent shepherd, but he's got an unaccountable bad dog!"

At the weddings of Sussex labourers, it was not the custom for the bride's father to give her away on her wedding day. Rather, the bridal procession consisted of the bride, the groom, the bridesmaid and the old father, who was usually the sweetheart of the bridesmaid (if she was single). It was the old father's responsibility to give the bride away at the ceremony.

Grave diggers or sextons performed a grim but necessary duty as part of church life, and they had a sense of humour all their own. When one old man was asked how deep he dug his graves, he thought for a moment and then replied, "Them as I don't like, I puts down another two feet so they'll be late for the resurrection."

In the village of Three Bridges, near Crawley, one of the village lads decided to dress up and frighten the local grave diggers on New Year's Eve. He donned a long white nightdress and applied liberal amounts of flour to his face and then lay in wait for the sextons as they passed through the churchyard. When he appeared, however, far from being terrified the old men simply regarded him calmly.

"Who do you rackon that is, then?" enquired one digger of the other.

"I dunno," replied the second old man, "but it ain't one o' mine. I allus digs mine in praper."

The following inscription may be found on a brass in Selmeston church, dated 1639:

The body of Henry Rogers.
A painfull preacher in this church
Two and thirty yeeres.

Another erstwhile denizen of Sussex is memorialised on his headstone in a highly individual and characteristically Sussex way:

Long was my pain, great was my grief.
Surgeons I'd many but no relief.
I trust through Christ to rise with the just.
My leg and thigh was buried fust.

Sundays were kept free of work and other responsibilities; the most someone might do would be to go out for a walk to see if anything could be found for supper – perhaps a rabbit or a pheasant. On their return, they might be asked, "Where bin 'day, then?"

"Oh, I just bin soodlin' up round Poke's Bottom, had a scoon about an' come back 'ome."

Old Uncle Tom was a local character who lived in Slinfold, near Horsham. His wife, Aunt Hannah, insisted that he should go to church every Sunday, which he did with some reluctance, sitting snoring in the pew known as Cadger's Row until he was woken by the verger.

One Sunday he didn't go, deciding to go hunting for hazel nuts on nearby farmland instead. He was spotted by the farmer, who accosted him.

"If you were in church, you wouldn't be stealin' my nuts!" he pointed out angrily.

Tom was unabashed. "Well," he replied, "if you was in church you wouldn't have seen me!"

St Martin's Church in the hamlet of Westmeston, near Ditchling, was commenced in the early twelfth century, and a local story tells of a farmer who contributed to the new building in a most unlikely way.

In the late eleventh century the tenant of Westmeston Farm had taken his tithes to Lewes Priory, since at that time Lewes was the nearest place of worship. Having delivered his tithes he took a walk along the river bank, whereupon he spied a barge coming to the landing stage laden with stone.

The bargee called, "Stone for Westminster new church!" (At that time the old St Peter's Abbey in London was being remodelled into Westminster Abbey by Edward the Confessor.) "I be from Westmeston!" called the farmer in reply.

"Then it must be for you!" called back the bargee. So the farmer brought up his waggon and they loaded the stone.

As he made his way back home he thought of what he had done, and was greatly afeared, so he laid the stones in the rickyard and rebuilt his ricks upon them, and no more was said or done about it.

However, it preyed on his conscience. Some years later, in 1099, the clerk to Lewes Priory came to assess for tithe, and he said to the farmer, "You and your family, all the villeins and boarders hereabouts, are a heathen lot according to the Prior, always missing mass. A church must be built here."

"Oh-ah," says the farmer. "I can supply one load o' stone." So the little church of St Martin in Westmeston was started with stone meant for a far larger edifice.

The rector of St Nicholas' Church in Brighton wondered why the local fishermen did not come to church more often. When he questioned them, he received the following answer:

"Well, sir, it be too far up the hill."

The rector was amused by this, and asked the fishermen if they would prefer the church brought to them. After some serious discussion among themselves the fishermen agreed that this was a good idea, and asked if they might slide the church down the hill on their boat rollers.

The rector laughed and said they might try, whereupon a gang of them went up the hill with the levers and slides they used for moving their boats up and down the beach.

Removing their coats and placing them on the ground in front of the church, they put their rollers in position and went behind the building to work with their levers.

A few minutes later a man walked along the road, and seeing all the coats on the ground in front of the church he collected them up and made off with them. A short time later one of the fishermen, red-faced and perspiring, came round to the front to check progress.

"Whoa!" he yelled. "We 'ave been and slid 'er on our coats! We'll 'ave to get 'er back!"

Bibliography

Many writers have celebrated and preserved the Sussex dialect, and as a consequence there is a wide variety of resources available. The first and most important is William Parish's wonderful Dictionary of the Sussex Dialect, which is a joy to read and return to, but all the books mentioned below were valuable sources of words and anecdotes for this book.

Arscott, D., Wunt Be Druv! (Countryside Books, 2006)

Candlin, L., Tales of Old Sussex (Countryside Books, 1985)

Collins, S., A Sussex Miscellany (Snake River Press, 2007)

Copper, B., Songs and Southern Breezes (Heinemann, 1973)

Gibbons, S., Cold Comfort Farm (Penguin Classics, 2006)

Moore, J., Silly Sussex (SB Publications, 2004)

Parish, W.D., A Dictionary of the Sussex Dialect (1875; reissued, Snake River Press, 2008)

Wales, T., Sussex Tales of Mirth and Mayhem (Countryside Books, 2001)

Wales, T., Sussex As She Wus Spoke (SB Publications, 2000)

Wymer, N., Companion into Sussex (Methuen, 1950)